"The Visionary" Dr. Baba Saheb Ambedkar
Unraveling the Legacy of India's Social Reformer

by

Ashok M

Double9 BOOKS

"The Visionary" Dr. Baba Saheb Ambedkar

Unraveling the Legacy of India's Social Reformer

by Ashok M

ISBN: 978-93-63058-23-1

Published by

DOUBLE 9 BOOKS

2/13-B, Ansari Road
Daryaganj, New Delhi – 110002
info@double9books.com
www.double9books.com
Tel. 011-40042856

ABOUT THE AUTHOR

Ashok M is a talented and versatile individual known for his remarkable contributions as an Author, Poet, Novelist, Philosopher, Entrepreneur and Government Official(Branch Manager at State Bank of India(SBI Bank), Posted in Jaipur). With a deep passion for literature and a profound understanding of the written word, he has created a name for himself in the literary world. Born with a natural inclination towards storytelling and a love for language, Ashok M began his writing journey at a young age. His innate creativity and vivid imagination allowed him to craft engaging narratives and powerful poems that resonated with readers across various genres. As an author, Ashok M has a unique ability to capture the essence of human emotions and experiences, transporting his readers into captivating worlds and thought-provoking scenarios. Whether through his novels, short stories, or poetry, he expertly weaves together compelling characters and evocative settings, leaving a lasting impact on his audience. In addition to his literary pursuits, Ashok M is also the Founder and CEO of Poetralia, a prominent platform dedicated to promoting and celebrating the art of poetry. With a vision to inspire and nurture emerging poets, he has created a vibrant community that encourages creativity and provides a platform for aspiring writers to share their work. Under his leadership, Poetralia has grown into a thriving hub for poets from all walks of life, fostering a supportive environment where artists can connect, collaborate, and showcase their talents. Through Poetralia, Ashok M has helped countless poets find their voice and gain recognition in the literary landscape. Beyond his literary achievements, Mr. Ashok M is known for his humility and commitment to empowering others. He actively mentors aspiring writers and poets, sharing his knowledge and expertise to guide them on their own creative journeys. His dedication to nurturing talent and fostering a love for literature has earned him respect and admiration among his peers. With a rich body of work and an unwavering passion for the written word, Ashok M continues to inspire and captivate readers with his literary prowess. His contributions to the world of literature and his commitment to supporting emerging poets through Poetralia make him a prominent figure in the literary community. As he continues to write, create, and empower others, Ashok M's influence on the world of words is set to grow even further.

CONTENTS

Introduction

In the vast tapestry of human history, certain individuals emerge as towering figures whose influence transcends their time and place. Dr. B.R. Ambedkar, affectionately known as Babasaheb, stands as a colossus among them. His life's journey was not just a personal odyssey but a relentless crusade for justice, equality, and dignity for the marginalized and oppressed. In the annals of social reform, his name shines brightly as a beacon of hope and inspiration.

Born into the depths of social inequality and oppression, Dr. Ambedkar faced myriad obstacles from his earliest days. Discrimination and prejudice were the harsh realities of his existence, yet he refused to succumb to despair. Instead, he resolved to challenge the entrenched systems of caste-based discrimination and untouchability that had shackled millions for centuries.

This book is a humble attempt to delve into the depths of Dr. Ambedkar's remarkable life—a life marked by resilience, determination, and unwavering commitment to the cause of social justice. Through meticulous research and heartfelt reflection, we aim to unravel the complexities of his journey, to shed light on his visionary ideas, and to celebrate his enduring legacy.

From his pioneering efforts in the field of education to his pivotal role in drafting the Indian Constitution, Dr. Ambedkar's contributions to society are manifold and profound. Yet, perhaps his greatest legacy lies in his unwavering belief in the inherent dignity and equality of all human beings—a belief that continues to inspire generations long after his passing.

As we embark on this journey of exploration and discovery, let us not only celebrate the life of Dr. B.R. Ambedkar but also reflect on the timeless lessons he imparts to us. In a world still plagued by injustice and inequality, his message of hope and empowerment resonates more strongly than ever.

Join us as we delve into the life, the legacy, and the enduring spirit of Babasaheb Ambedkar—a true champion of the downtrodden, a tireless advocate for social reform, and a guiding light for all who strive for a more just and equitable world.

Preface

Dr. B.R. Ambedkar's life epitomizes the triumph of the human spirit against all odds. His struggles, sacrifices, and triumphs serve as a beacon of hope for millions around the globe. This book seeks to unravel the multifaceted persona of Babasaheb, shedding light on his visionary ideas, socio-political activism, and enduring impact on modern India.

Acknowledgement

I extend my heartfelt gratitude to all those who have contributed to this endeavor. To the scholars, researchers, and historians whose works have illuminated the life of Dr. B.R. Ambedkar, I owe a debt of gratitude. To my family, friends, and mentors whose unwavering support has been my guiding light, thank you. This book is dedicated to the memory of Babasaheb, whose legacy continues to inspire generations.

Dedication

To always inspire, impart the lesson of diligence, and bestow affectionate blessings, and to dedicate oneself at the revered lotus feet of my beloved **mother, Shrimati Godavari Ji Devi**, and my revered **father, Shri Prabhu Dayal Ji Meghwal.** To the memory of Dr. B.R. Ambedkar, whose tireless efforts paved the way for a more just and equitable society. May his legacy continue to inspire us to strive for a world free from discrimination and prejudice.

Before delving into the rich tapestry of Dr. B.R. Ambedkar's life and legacy, let us embark on a journey that traverses the realms of history, courage, and transformation. Brace yourself for an odyssey through the corridors of time, where the footsteps of a visionary echo with the resonance of change. Prepare to be captivated by the extraordinary saga of a man who defied the odds, shattered barriers, and illuminated the path to a brighter future for generations to come.

As we turn the pages of this book, let us immerse ourselves in the compelling narrative of Dr. B.R. Ambedkar—a narrative that transcends the boundaries of caste, creed, and convention, weaving together the threads of resilience, intellect, and compassion. From his humble beginnings in a small town to his towering presence on the global stage, Dr. Ambedkar's life story is a testament to the power of determination, courage, and unwavering commitment to justice.

So, dear reader, fasten your seatbelt and prepare to embark on an exhilarating voyage—one that will take you on a rollercoaster ride of emotions, insights, and revelations. For within the pages of this book lies the untold story of a visionary leader whose life's work continues to shape the destiny of nations and inspire millions around the world. Welcome to the world of Dr. B.R. Ambedkar—a world of passion, purpose, and possibility.

Chapter 1
Early Years

Dr. B.R. Ambedkar's journey from his humble beginnings to becoming the architect of India's Constitution is a testament to the power of resilience and determination. Born on April 14, 1891, in the town of Mhow, now in Madhya Pradesh, Babasaheb entered a world deeply entrenched in the rigid hierarchies of the caste system.

From his earliest days, young Bhimrao faced the harsh realities of discrimination and social exclusion. As a member of the Dalit community, he was subjected to indignities and injustices that would shape his worldview and fuel his lifelong commitment to social reform.Despite the obstacles he faced, Bhimrao displayed an insatiable thirst for knowledge from a young age. Encouraged by his father, Ramji Maloji Sakpal, a retired army officer, he embarked on a journey of intellectual exploration that would take him far beyond the confines of his upbringing.

In 1897, tragedy struck the family when Bhimrao's mother, Bhimabai, passed away. This loss, coupled with the pervasive discrimination he experienced, deepened his resolve to challenge the status quo and fight for the rights of the oppressed.

Babasaheb's early education was marked by struggles and setbacks. Denied entry into local schools due to his caste, he was forced to seek education under challenging circumstances. However, his indomitable spirit and determination led him to overcome these obstacles, eventually earning a scholarship to study at Elphinstone High School in Bombay (now Mumbai).

At Elphinstone, Bhimrao distinguished himself as a brilliant student, excelling in academics and extracurricular activities alike. His intellectual prowess caught the attention of his teachers and peers, laying the foundation for his future academic pursuits.

Despite his academic success, Bhimrao's journey was fraught with hardship. He faced discrimination at every turn, from being forced to sit on the floor in classrooms to being denied access to drinking water. These experiences served as a stark reminder of the pervasive inequality that defined Indian society at the time.

Undeterred by these challenges, Bhimrao continued to pursue his education with unwavering determination. After completing his schooling, he enrolled at Elphinstone College, where he earned a Bachelor's degree in Economics and Political Science, laying the groundwork for his future endeavors in law and social reform.

Babasaheb's formative years were marked by a deepening awareness of the injustices faced by Dalits and other marginalized communities. His encounters with caste-based discrimination fueled his commitment to social justice, planting the seeds of activism that would define his life's work.

As we reflect on the early years of Dr. B.R. Ambedkar, we are reminded of the transformative power of education, resilience, and unwavering determination. From his humble beginnings in Mhow to his academic pursuits in Bombay and beyond, Babasaheb's journey serves as an inspiration to all who dare to challenge injustice and strive for a more equitable world.

"I measure the progress of a community by the degree of progress which women have achieved." - BR Ambedkar

Dr. B.R. Ambedkar's personal life was as remarkable as his public achievements, marked by challenges and triumphs that shaped his journey as a social reformer and leader. Here's a glimpse into his family, marriage, wife, and children:

Family Background:

Born on April 14, 1891, in the town of Mhow in present-day Madhya Pradesh, Bhimrao Ramji Ambedkar was the fourteenth and youngest child of Ramji Maloji Sakpal and Bhimabai Maloji Sakpal. His family belonged to the Mahar caste, considered "untouchable" and subjected to severe social discrimination and oppression under the caste system.

Marriage:

Dr. Ambedkar's marriage to Dr. Ramabai Ambedkar, also known as Ramabai Bhimrao Ambedkar or Mai, was a significant milestone in his life. Ramabai, a qualified medical professional, was the daughter of a prominent social reformer, Bhikaji Cama. The marriage took place in 1906 when Ambedkar was only 15 years old, and Ramabai was 9. This child marriage was arranged by their families, a common practice at the time.

Family Life:

Ambedkar's marriage to Ramabai faced numerous challenges, including financial difficulties and societal prejudice against their inter-caste union. Despite these hardships, the couple remained devoted to each other and supported each other's aspirations and endeavors.

Children:

Dr. Ambedkar and Ramabai had five children together:

1. Yashwant (Bhaiyasaheb) Ambedkar
2. Gangadhar (Dattu) Ambedkar
3. Ramesh (Baba) Ambedkar
4. Indu (Maisaheb) Ambedkar
5. Rajratna Ambedkar

Their children faced the dual burden of belonging to a marginalized community and being the offspring of a renowned social reformer, navigating societal expectations and challenges while striving to uphold their father's legacy.

Despite the complexities of their personal lives, Dr. B.R. Ambedkar and Ramabai remained committed to their shared vision of social reform and equality. Their partnership, marked by mutual respect, resilience, and unwavering dedication to the cause of justice, serves as a testament to the enduring power of love and solidarity in the face of adversity.

Chapter 2
Education and Enlightenment

Dr. B.R. Ambedkar's pursuit of education was not merely a quest for personal advancement but a journey towards enlightenment and empowerment. His relentless efforts to overcome the barriers of caste-based discrimination and unequal access to education laid the groundwork for his transformative impact on Indian society.

From his early struggles for equal education in colonial India to his pursuit of higher learning abroad, Babasaheb's educational journey was marked by perseverance, resilience, and a steadfast commitment to knowledge.

Denied equal opportunities for education due to his caste, Bhimrao faced formidable obstacles in his quest for learning. Despite these challenges, he refused to be deterred and resolved to challenge the entrenched system of discrimination that denied millions of Dalits their right to education.

Babasaheb's academic pursuits took him to the United States, where he enrolled at Columbia University to pursue a graduate degree in Economics. It was here that he was exposed to new ideas and intellectual currents that would shape his worldview and inform his future activism.

During his time at Columbia, Dr. Ambedkar immersed himself in the study of economics, sociology, and political science, exploring the root causes of social inequality and injustice. He engaged with leading scholars and thinkers of the time, including John Dewey and Edwin R.A. Seligman, whose ideas on democracy and social reform left a lasting impression on him.

Upon completing his studies at Columbia, Babasaheb traveled to England to further his education at the University of London. Here, he earned multiple degrees, including a doctorate in Economics, Law, and Political Science, becoming one of the first Dalits to attain such academic distinctions.

His time in England exposed him to the principles of liberty, equality, and fraternity espoused by the European Enlightenment thinkers, as well as the nascent movements for social justice and civil rights taking shape across the Western world. Inspired by these ideals, Dr. Ambedkar returned to India with a renewed sense of purpose and a burning desire to challenge the injustices of the caste system.

The intellectual influences that shaped Dr. Ambedkar's worldview were diverse and eclectic, ranging from Western liberalism to Indian traditions of social reform. His synthesis of these ideas culminated in his visionary vision of a society based on equality, justice, and human dignity.

As we trace Dr. Ambedkar's journey through academia, we are reminded of the transformative power of education to challenge prejudice, broaden perspectives, and empower individuals to effect meaningful change. His quest for knowledge was not merely an intellectual pursuit but a revolutionary act of defiance against the oppressive forces of caste-based discrimination and social injustice.

In uncovering the intellectual influences that shaped Babasaheb's worldview, we gain insight into the foundations of his lifelong commitment to social reform and his unwavering dedication to the cause of equality and justice for all.

Some Fascinating Facts About Dr. Bhimrao Ambedkar

1. Architect of the Indian Constitution: Dr. Ambedkar played a pivotal role in drafting the Constitution of India. He chaired the Drafting Committee and was instrumental in ensuring that it reflected principles of social justice, equality, and fundamental rights.

2. First Law Minister of Independent India: He served as the first Law Minister of independent India from 1947 to 1951 in Jawaharlal Nehru's cabinet. During his tenure, he introduced several landmark legislations aimed at social reform and equality.

3. Champion of Social Reform: Dr. Ambedkar dedicated his life to the upliftment of the marginalized and oppressed communities, particularly the Dalits (formerly known as "untouchables"). He fought against caste-based discrimination and advocated for their rights and dignity.

4. Education Advocate: Dr. Ambedkar emphasized the importance of education as a means of empowerment. He himself faced immense challenges in pursuing education due to caste-based discrimination but eventually earned multiple degrees, including a doctorate from Columbia University in the United States.

5. Iconic Statue: The iconic statue of Dr. Ambedkar, popularly known as the "Ambedkar Statue of Equality," stands tall in Hyderabad, India. It is one of the tallest statues of Dr. Ambedkar in the world, symbolizing his enduring legacy and contribution to social justice.

6. Conversion to Buddhism: In 1956, Dr. Ambedkar embraced Buddhism along with thousands of his followers in a historic mass conversion ceremony in Nagpur, India. This conversion was a symbolic rejection of the caste system and a reaffirmation of the principles of equality and social justice.

7. International Influence: Dr. Ambedkar's ideas and activism have had a significant impact beyond India. He is studied and admired by scholars and activists worldwide for his contributions to social justice, human rights, and anti-discrimination movements.

8. Awarded Bharat Ratna: In 1990, Dr. Bhimrao Ambedkar was posthumously conferred with India's highest civilian award, the Bharat Ratna, in recognition of his exceptional service to the nation and his tireless efforts towards social reform and upliftment of the downtrodden.

Chapter 3
The Architect of the Indian Constitution

Ambedkar's pivotal role in drafting the Indian Constitution stands as a testament to his unwavering commitment to justice, equality, and democracy. As the chairman of the Drafting Committee, Babasaheb played a central role in shaping the foundational document of independent India, championing the cause of fundamental rights and social justice.

Amidst the backdrop of a newly independent nation grappling with the legacies of colonialism and social inequality, Dr. Ambedkar emerged as a towering figure in the Constituent Assembly—a beacon of hope for millions of marginalized and oppressed Indians.

From the outset, Babasaheb approached the task of drafting the Constitution with a clear vision and a deep sense of purpose. He sought to create a document that would not only establish the framework for governance but also enshrine the principles of justice, liberty, and equality as the cornerstone of the new Indian republic.

Central to Dr. Ambedkar's vision was the inclusion of fundamental rights that would guarantee every citizen the right to equality before the law, freedom of speech and expression, and protection from discrimination based on caste, religion, or gender. These rights, he believed, were essential for safeguarding the dignity and autonomy of individuals in a democratic society.

Throughout the drafting process, Babasaheb faced numerous challenges and obstacles, both from within the Constituent Assembly and from external forces opposed to his progressive agenda. His impassioned advocacy for the rights of Dalits, women, and other marginalized communities often put him at odds with more conservative members of the Assembly, who sought to preserve the status quo.

Despite these challenges, Dr. Ambedkar remained steadfast in his commitment to social justice, tirelessly arguing for the inclusion of provisions that would protect the rights of the oppressed and ensure their full participation in the democratic process.

One of the most contentious issues during the drafting of the Constitution was the question of reservations for disadvantaged groups in educational institutions and government jobs. Dr. Ambedkar fiercely defended the principle of affirmative action, arguing that it was necessary to address historical injustices and ensure the equitable representation of all sections of society.

In the end, Dr. Ambedkar's efforts bore fruit with the adoption of a Constitution that reflected his progressive vision for India—a vision that embraced diversity, protected individual liberties, and guaranteed social justice for all.

As we examine Dr. Ambedkar's pivotal role in drafting the Indian Constitution, we are reminded of his enduring legacy as a champion of democracy and human rights. His tireless advocacy for fundamental rights and social justice continues to inspire generations of Indians to strive for a more inclusive and equitable society—one that upholds the principles of liberty, equality, and fraternity for all its citizens.

> **"Law and order are the medicine of the body politic and when the body politic gets sick, medicine must be administered."**

Chapter 4
Champion of Dalit Rights

B.R. Ambedkar's life was synonymous with the relentless struggle against caste-based discrimination and untouchability. Throughout his career, he spearheaded numerous movements and initiatives aimed at empowering the Dalit community and eradicating the deep-rooted prejudices that pervaded Indian society.

One of the earliest manifestations of Babasaheb's commitment to the cause of Dalit rights was the historic Mahad Satyagraha of 1927. Frustrated by the denial of access to public water sources for Dalits, Dr. Ambedkar led a peaceful protest in Mahad, Maharashtra, demanding the right to use the town's public tank. The Satyagraha marked a watershed moment in the struggle against untouchability, challenging centuries-old social norms and asserting the dignity and rights of the oppressed.

The Mahad Satyagraha was followed by another seminal event in the history of Dalit empowerment—the signing of the Poona Pact in 1932. In response to the British government's decision to grant separate electorates for Dalits, Babasaheb negotiated with Mahatma Gandhi to secure greater political representation for the Dalit community within the framework of a unified electorate system. The Poona Pact represented a significant victory for Dr. Ambedkar and marked a crucial step towards ensuring Dalit participation in the political process.

Throughout his life, Babasaheb recognized the transformative power of education in emancipating the oppressed and marginalized. He dedicated himself to promoting education among Dalits, establishing schools and educational institutions to provide them with opportunities for intellectual and social upliftment. For Dr. Ambedkar, education was not merely a means to acquire knowledge but a tool for liberation—a path to empowerment and self-realization for those trapped in the chains of caste-based oppression.

In addition to his advocacy for education and political representation, Dr. Ambedkar was a tireless crusader for social reform. He sought to challenge the entrenched hierarchies of caste and dismantle the oppressive structures that relegated Dalits to the margins of society. Through his writings, speeches, and activism, Babasaheb called for a radical reimagining of Indian society—one based on the principles of equality, justice, and human dignity.

The legacy of Dr. B.R. Ambedkar as a champion of Dalit rights continues to resonate today, inspiring generations of activists and reformers to carry forward his unfinished agenda. His unwavering commitment to social justice, his courage in the face of adversity, and his tireless efforts to empower the marginalized have left an indelible mark on the fabric of Indian society. As we reflect on his legacy, we are reminded of the enduring importance of standing up against injustice and fighting for the rights of all oppressed communities.

> **"History shows that where ethics and economics come in conflict, victory is always with economics. Vested interests have never been known to have willingly divested themselves unless there was sufficient force to compel them."**

Chapter 5
Emancipation of Women

Dr. B.R. Ambedkar's vision of social justice extended beyond caste-based discrimination to encompass gender inequality as well. Throughout his life, Babasaheb was a staunch advocate for the emancipation of women, recognizing their inherent dignity and rights as equal members of society. His progressive views on gender equality and his pioneering efforts to empower women have left a lasting legacy in the annals of Indian history.

At the heart of Dr. Ambedkar's advocacy for women's rights was his unwavering belief in the principle of equality. He saw gender discrimination as a pervasive social evil that perpetuated injustice and hindered the progress of society as a whole. In his writings and speeches, Babasaheb challenged traditional patriarchal norms and called for a radical reevaluation of gender roles and relations.

One of Dr. Ambedkar's most significant contributions to the emancipation of women was his role in shaping the legal framework of independent India. As the chairman of the Drafting Committee of the Indian Constitution, he played a key role in ensuring that the Constitution enshrined the principles of gender equality and women's rights. The inclusion of provisions such as equal rights under the law, non-discrimination on the basis of gender, and affirmative action for women marked a historic milestone in the struggle for gender justice.

Beyond his work on the Constitution, Dr. Ambedkar was actively involved in advocating for legal reforms to protect women from exploitation and abuse. He championed laws against child marriage, dowry, and other harmful practices that oppressed women and girls. Babasaheb recognized that legal reforms were essential but not sufficient; they must be accompanied by social and cultural changes to truly emancipate women from oppression.

Education was another cornerstone of Dr. Ambedkar's strategy for the empowerment of women. He believed that access to education was key to breaking the cycle of poverty and ignorance that trapped many women in oppressive social structures. Babasaheb advocated for the establishment of schools and colleges for girls and women, providing them with the tools they needed to assert their rights and pursue their aspirations.

In addition to legal reforms and education, Dr. Ambedkar also promoted economic empowerment as a means of achieving gender equality. He recognized the importance of economic independence in enabling women to exercise control over their lives and make meaningful contributions to society. Babasaheb advocated for policies that would ensure women's access to employment, land ownership, and financial resources, empowering them to chart their own destinies free from economic dependence.

As we reflect on Dr. Ambedkar's legacy in the emancipation of women, we are reminded of his enduring commitment to the principles of equality, justice, and human dignity. His visionary leadership continues to inspire generations of women and men to strive for a more equitable and inclusive society—one where gender equality is not just a distant dream but a lived reality for all.

Chapter 6
Economic Vision

Dr. B.R. Ambedkar's economic vision for India was rooted in the principles of social justice, equitable distribution of resources, and empowerment of the marginalized communities. As an economist and social reformer, Babasaheb recognized the pivotal role of economic development in lifting millions out of poverty and transforming Indian society.

At the heart of Dr. Ambedkar's economic vision was the imperative of land reforms to address the deep-seated inequalities in agrarian society. He advocated for the redistribution of land from large landowners to landless peasants and tenant farmers, believing that landownership was essential for ensuring economic security and social mobility for the rural poor. Babasaheb saw land reforms as a means of breaking the stranglehold of feudalism and empowering the most marginalized sections of society.

In addition to land reforms, Dr. Ambedkar championed industrialization as a catalyst for economic growth and development. He recognized the need for a diversified economy that would create employment opportunities and generate wealth for all segments of society. Babasaheb advocated for state intervention in key sectors of the economy to promote industrial growth and foster entrepreneurship, particularly among the Dalit and other marginalized communities.

Central to Dr. Ambedkar's economic vision was the concept of social welfare policies aimed at uplifting the disadvantaged sections of society. He believed that the state had a moral obligation to provide for the basic needs of its citizens, including food, shelter, healthcare, and education. Babasaheb advocated for the establishment of social security programs, public healthcare systems, and universal education initiatives to ensure that no one was left behind in the march towards progress and prosperity.

Dr. Ambedkar's economic vision was characterized by a holistic approach that sought to address the root causes of poverty and inequality. He recognized that economic development alone was not sufficient to achieve social justice; it must be accompanied by social and political reforms that empower the marginalized and ensure their full participation in the decision-making process.

As we unravel Dr. Ambedkar's economic vision for India, we are reminded of his unwavering commitment to building a society based on equality, justice, and human dignity. His pioneering ideas on land reforms, industrialization, and social welfare continue to resonate today, inspiring policymakers and activists to strive for a more inclusive and equitable economic system—one that uplifts the marginalized and empowers all citizens to realize their full potential.

Chapter 7
Legacy of Annihilation of Caste

Dr. B.R. Ambedkar's seminal work, "Annihilation of Caste," stands as a powerful critique of the caste system and a clarion call for radical social reform. Published in 1936 as the keynote address for a conference organized by the Jat-Pat Todak Mandal, Babasaheb's impassioned indictment of caste-based discrimination continues to resonate in contemporary India, challenging entrenched prejudices and inspiring movements for social justice.

At the heart of "Annihilation of Caste" is Dr. Ambedkar's uncompromising critique of the caste system as the most pernicious form of social hierarchy and inequality. He exposes caste as a system of social stratification that denies human beings their inherent dignity and deprives them of equal opportunities based solely on birth. Babasaheb deconstructs the myths and justifications used to perpetuate caste oppression, arguing that it is not only morally indefensible but also antithetical to the principles of democracy and human rights.

Dr. Ambedkar's critique of the caste system is rooted in his own experiences as a member of the Dalit community and his relentless struggle against caste-based discrimination. He exposes the insidious ways in which caste operates to maintain social control and perpetuate the privileges of the upper castes at the expense of the oppressed and marginalized. Babasaheb challenges the notion of caste as a divinely ordained order and calls for its annihilation as a precondition for building a truly democratic and egalitarian society.

Central to Dr. Ambedkar's argument in "Annihilation of Caste" is the need for radical social reform to dismantle the caste system and create a more just and equitable society. He calls for the abolition of caste-based distinctions in all spheres of life, including marriage, education, and employment. Babasaheb advocates for inter-caste marriage as a means of breaking down the barriers of caste and fostering social harmony and integration.

The enduring relevance of "Annihilation of Caste" lies in its uncompromising commitment to truth and justice. Dr. Ambedkar's searing critique of caste oppression continues to challenge the conscience of Indian society, forcing us to confront the deep-rooted prejudices and inequalities that persist to this day. His call for radical social reform echoes across the decades, inspiring movements for social justice and equality that seek to realize his vision of a casteless society.

As we reflect on the legacy of "Annihilation of Caste," we are reminded of Dr. Ambedkar's enduring relevance as a champion of human rights and social justice. His words remain a beacon of hope for all who strive for a world free from the shackles of caste oppression—a world where every individual is treated with dignity, respect, and equality, regardless of their caste or background.

Chapter 8
Political Legacy

Dr. B.R. Ambedkar's political journey is a testament to his unwavering commitment to social justice and his tireless efforts to empower the marginalized and oppressed sections of society. From his early leadership of the Independent Labour Party to his pivotal role as the first Law Minister of independent India, Babasaheb left an indelible mark on Indian politics, shaping the course of parliamentary democracy and championing the cause of the downtrodden.

Born out of the need to provide a political platform for the oppressed classes, the Independent Labour Party (ILP) was founded by Dr. Ambedkar in 1936. As its leader, Babasaheb sought to mobilize Dalits and other marginalized communities to assert their political rights and demand social reform. The ILP became a vehicle for Dr. Ambedkar's advocacy for land reforms, abolition of untouchability, and representation of the oppressed in the political process.

Dr. Ambedkar's political acumen and unwavering commitment to social justice earned him recognition as a formidable leader and a voice for the voiceless. His advocacy for the rights of Dalits and other marginalized communities resonated with millions across the country, galvanizing support for his vision of a more inclusive and equitable society.

In 1947, with the dawn of independence, Dr. Ambedkar was appointed as the Law Minister in the interim government of India, headed by Prime Minister Jawaharlal Nehru. As the principal architect of the Indian Constitution, Babasaheb played a central role in shaping the legal framework of the newly independent nation. His keen understanding of constitutional law and his commitment to democratic principles were instrumental in crafting a document that enshrined the ideals of equality, justice, and liberty for all citizens.

One of Dr. Ambedkar's most significant contributions to Indian politics was his advocacy for affirmative action for the oppressed classes. He fought tirelessly for the inclusion of provisions in the Constitution that would provide for reservations in educational institutions and government jobs for Dalits, Scheduled Castes, and Scheduled Tribes. These affirmative action policies, commonly known as "reservation," have since become a cornerstone of India's social justice framework, empowering millions of marginalized individuals to access opportunities for education and employment.

Dr. Ambedkar's political legacy extends beyond his contributions to the Constitution to encompass his advocacy for social reform and his commitment to building a more just and equitable society. His ideas on parliamentary democracy, social justice, and human rights continue to shape the political discourse in India, inspiring generations of leaders and activists to work towards the realization of his vision.

As we trace Dr. Ambedkar's political journey, we are reminded of his enduring impact on Indian politics and society. His leadership, advocacy, and unwavering commitment to social justice continue to serve as a guiding light for all who strive for a more inclusive and equitable world.

Chapter 9
International Influence

Dr. B.R. Ambedkar's engagements with the international community were marked by his relentless advocacy for minority rights, social justice, and human dignity on the global stage. From his participation in the Round Table Conferences to his leadership in international forums, Babasaheb left an indelible mark on the discourse of human rights and equality worldwide.

In the 1930s, Dr. Ambedkar emerged as a prominent voice representing the interests of the oppressed classes of India in the international arena. He participated in the Round Table Conferences convened by the British government to discuss constitutional reforms for India. Babasaheb used these platforms to highlight the plight of Dalits and other marginalized communities and to advocate for their inclusion in the political process.

Dr. Ambedkar's engagements with the international community were not limited to the political sphere; he also sought to raise awareness about the social and economic injustices faced by the oppressed classes in India. Babasaheb's writings and speeches on caste-based discrimination and untouchability resonated with audiences around the world, drawing attention to the pervasive nature of caste oppression and its impact on millions of lives.

One of Dr. Ambedkar's key contributions to the international discourse on human rights was his advocacy for minority rights and social justice. He emphasized the importance of recognizing and protecting the rights of minorities, including religious, ethnic, and caste minorities, as a fundamental principle of democracy and pluralism. Babasaheb's insights into the complexities of minority rights continue to inform discussions on diversity and inclusion in today's globalized world.

In addition to his advocacy work, Dr. Ambedkar also engaged with international organizations and institutions to promote social justice and equality. He participated in conferences and seminars organized by the United Nations and other international bodies, where he spoke passionately about the need for concerted action to address the root causes of inequality and discrimination.

Dr. Ambedkar's international influence extended beyond his lifetime, inspiring generations of activists and leaders around the world to champion the cause of social justice and human rights. His ideas on minority rights, social reform, and democratic governance continue to resonate in the global struggle for equality and dignity for all.

As we explore Dr. Ambedkar's engagements with the international community, we are reminded of his enduring legacy as a champion of human rights and social justice. His advocacy for the oppressed and marginalized transcended national boundaries, leaving an indelible mark on the global struggle for equality and dignity for all.

Chapter 10
Educational Reformer

Dr. B.R. Ambedkar's vision for education was deeply rooted in his belief that knowledge is the key to social transformation and empowerment. Throughout his life, Babasaheb worked tirelessly to promote education among the marginalized and oppressed communities, recognizing it as a powerful tool for breaking the chains of caste-based oppression and fostering social mobility.

One of Dr. Ambedkar's most significant contributions to education was the establishment of the People's Education Society (PES) in 1945. Founded with the aim of providing quality education to the economically and socially disadvantaged sections of society, the PES became a vehicle for Babasaheb's vision of educational empowerment. Under his leadership, the society established schools, colleges, and vocational training centers across India, providing thousands of students from marginalized backgrounds with access to educational opportunities previously denied to them.

Dr. Ambedkar's commitment to education was not limited to primary and secondary schooling; he also recognized the importance of higher education in fostering leadership and intellectual development among the oppressed classes. Babasaheb advocated for the establishment of universities and colleges specifically for Dalits and other marginalized communities, where they could receive quality education free from discrimination and prejudice.

One of the most enduring legacies of Dr. Ambedkar's educational reforms is the establishment of the Dr. Babasaheb Ambedkar Open University in Gujarat. Founded in 1994, the university aims to provide distance education opportunities to students who are unable to attend traditional brick-and-mortar institutions due to social, economic, or geographical constraints. The university's flexible learning programs enable thousands of students from diverse backgrounds to pursue higher education and enhance their skills and knowledge.

In addition to his efforts to expand access to education, Dr. Ambedkar also advocated for reforms within the educational system to make it more inclusive and equitable. He called for the eradication of caste-based discrimination in schools and colleges, as well as the promotion of curriculum that reflects the diversity of Indian society and promotes social justice and equality.

Dr. Ambedkar's vision for education as a tool for social transformation continues to inspire educators, policymakers, and activists around the world. His tireless advocacy for educational empowerment and his unwavering commitment to the cause of equality and justice serve as a beacon of hope for all who strive to build a more inclusive and equitable society.

As we explore Dr. Ambedkar's legacy as an educational reformer, we are reminded of the transformative power of education to uplift individuals and communities, to challenge prejudice and discrimination, and to pave the way for a brighter and more equitable future for all.

Chapter 11
Iconic Symbol

Dr. B.R. Ambedkar's enduring legacy as an iconic symbol of social justice and equality is evident in the proliferation of his statues across India and the celebration of his birth anniversary as a national holiday. Babasaheb's life and teachings continue to inspire millions of people from diverse backgrounds, transcending boundaries of caste, religion, and nationality.

The proliferation of Dr. Ambedkar's statues across India is a testament to his enduring influence and popularity. From bustling cities to remote villages, statues of Babasaheb can be found in public squares, parks, and educational institutions, serving as a constant reminder of his contributions to the struggle for social justice and equality. These statues not only honor his memory but also serve as rallying points for activists and advocates working to uphold his ideals.

The celebration of Dr. Ambedkar's birth anniversary as a national holiday further underscores his significance as an iconic symbol of social justice and equality. Observed on April 14th every year, Ambedkar Jayanti is marked by various commemorative events, including seminars, lectures, cultural programs, and community gatherings. The day provides an opportunity for people from all walks of life to pay tribute to Babasaheb's legacy and reflect on the continuing relevance of his teachings in the contemporary world.

Dr. Ambedkar's iconic status extends beyond India's borders, with his teachings and activism inspiring social justice movements around the globe. From the United States to Africa to Europe, Babasaheb's ideas on caste, inequality, and human rights have found resonance among marginalized communities fighting for dignity and equality. His life's work continues to inspire individuals and groups to challenge injustice, advocate for equality, and strive for a more just and inclusive society.

In addition to statues and commemorative events, Dr. Ambedkar's legacy is preserved through various institutions, organizations, and initiatives dedicated to promoting his teachings and advancing the cause of social justice. Universities, research centers, and cultural institutions bear his name and carry forward his mission of empowering the oppressed and marginalized.

As we examine Dr. Ambedkar's enduring legacy as an iconic symbol of social justice and equality, we are reminded of the transformative power of his ideas and activism. His life's work continues to inspire millions of people around the world to stand up against injustice, to fight for equality and dignity for all, and to work towards building a more just and inclusive society.

Chapter 12
Challenges and Controversies

Dr. B.R. Ambedkar's life and legacy were marked by numerous challenges and controversies, reflecting the complex social and political landscape of his time. From his ideological battles with Mahatma Gandhi to the complexities of his relationship with the Indian National Congress, Babasaheb navigated a path fraught with obstacles and contradictions as he fought for the rights of the oppressed and marginalized.

One of the most prominent controversies in Dr. Ambedkar's life was his ideological differences with Mahatma Gandhi, particularly on the issue of caste and untouchability. While both leaders shared a commitment to social reform and fought against the injustices of colonial rule, they diverged on the methods and priorities of the struggle for social justice. Babasaheb criticized Gandhi's approach of appealing to the moral conscience of the oppressors, arguing that it did not address the structural inequalities perpetuated by the caste system. Gandhi, in turn, was skeptical of Ambedkar's demand for separate electorates for Dalits, fearing that it would further divide Indian society along caste lines. Despite their differences, both leaders recognized the need for dialogue and cooperation in the pursuit of common goals, and their interactions paved the way for significant reforms in the fight against untouchability.

Another source of controversy in Dr. Ambedkar's life was his relationship with the Indian National Congress (INC), the leading political party in the struggle for Indian independence. While Ambedkar collaborated with the Congress on various issues, including the drafting of the Indian Constitution, his relationship with the party was often strained by differences in ideology and strategy. Babasaheb criticized the Congress for its failure to adequately address the concerns of Dalits and other marginalized communities, accusing it of perpetuating the status quo of caste-based oppression. Despite his reservations, Dr. Ambedkar recognized the importance of political alliances in advancing the cause of social justice and worked with the Congress to secure protections for Dalits and other disadvantaged groups in the Constitution.

Throughout his life, Dr. Ambedkar faced challenges and controversies from both within and outside the Dalit community. His uncompromising stance on issues of caste and untouchability often put him at odds with traditionalists and conservative elements within Dalit society, who viewed his advocacy for social reform as a threat to their interests. Babasaheb also faced criticism from political opponents who sought to undermine his leadership and discredit his ideas. Despite these challenges, Dr. Ambedkar remained steadfast in his commitment to the cause of social justice and equality, tirelessly advocating for the rights of the oppressed and marginalized until his last breath.

As we confront the controversies and challenges that marked Dr. Ambedkar's life and legacy, we are reminded of the complexities of his role as a leader and reformer. Babasaheb's struggles against injustice and inequality continue to inspire generations of activists and advocates to confront the injustices of their time and strive for a more just and inclusive society.

Chapter 13
Dalit Movement Today

The Dalit movement in contemporary India stands as a testament to the enduring legacy of Dr. B.R. Ambedkar and his teachings on social justice, equality, and human dignity. Drawing inspiration from Babasaheb's vision and activism, the Dalit movement continues to confront the ongoing challenges of caste-based discrimination and social exclusion, advocating for the rights and empowerment of the oppressed and marginalized communities.

Despite significant progress since independence, caste-based discrimination and social exclusion remain pervasive in Indian society, affecting millions of Dalits and other marginalized groups. The Dalit movement today seeks to address these entrenched inequalities by mobilizing communities, raising awareness, and advocating for systemic change.

At the heart of the Dalit movement is the principle of assertion and empowerment, inspired by Dr. Ambedkar's call for self-respect and dignity. Dalit activists and leaders across India are reclaiming their identity and heritage, challenging centuries-old prejudices and stereotypes, and asserting their right to equality and justice.

One of the key strategies of the Dalit movement is political mobilization and representation. Dalit political parties and leaders are working to ensure that the voices and concerns of marginalized communities are heard in the corridors of power. Through electoral politics, Dalit leaders are advocating for policies and programs that address the specific needs of Dalits and other marginalized groups, including affirmative action, land reforms, and social welfare initiatives.

Education also plays a crucial role in the Dalit movement, echoing Dr. Ambedkar's belief in the transformative power of knowledge. Dalit activists and organizations are working to improve access to education for Dalit children, eradicate caste-based discrimination in schools and colleges, and promote awareness of Dalit history and culture. By empowering Dalit youth with education and skills, the movement seeks to break the cycle of poverty and exclusion and pave the way for a brighter future.

The Dalit movement today is also leveraging technology and media to amplify its message and reach a wider audience. Social media platforms, online campaigns, and digital storytelling are being used to raise awareness about caste-based discrimination, highlight instances of injustice, and mobilize support for the cause of social justice.

Despite the challenges and obstacles that remain, the Dalit movement draws strength from Dr. Ambedkar's teachings and legacy, inspiring hope and resilience among millions of marginalized individuals. Babasaheb's vision of a casteless society based on equality, justice, and human dignity continues to guide the movement as it confronts the entrenched forces of casteism and discrimination.

As we assess the state of the Dalit movement in contemporary India, we are reminded of the enduring relevance of Dr. Ambedkar's teachings and the ongoing struggle for social justice and equality. The Dalit movement stands as a beacon of hope for all who believe in the inherent dignity and worth of every human being, and its journey towards liberation and empowerment continues to inspire generations to come.

Chapter 14
Global Reverberations

Dr. B.R. Ambedkar's ideas and legacy have reverberated far beyond the shores of India, leaving an indelible mark on the global struggle for social justice and human rights. From the spread of the Dalit diaspora to the growing recognition of his contributions to social justice worldwide, Babasaheb's influence continues to resonate across continents and cultures.

The spread of the Dalit diaspora is one of the most visible manifestations of Dr. Ambedkar's global impact. Over the years, millions of Dalits have migrated from India to various parts of the world, seeking opportunities for education, employment, and a better life. The diaspora has formed vibrant communities in countries such as the United States, the United Kingdom, Canada, and Australia, where Dalits have organized themselves to advocate for their rights and promote awareness of caste-based discrimination. Dr. Ambedkar's teachings and activism serve as a guiding light for the diaspora, inspiring them to assert their identity and fight for equality and dignity in their adopted homelands.

In addition to the Dalit diaspora, Dr. Ambedkar's ideas have also gained recognition and resonance among scholars, activists, and policymakers around the world. Babasaheb's pioneering work on caste, inequality, and social justice has been studied and celebrated in academic circles, leading to a growing appreciation of his contributions to the global discourse on human rights and equality. International conferences, seminars, and publications have sought to explore the relevance of Dr. Ambedkar's ideas in diverse cultural and political contexts, highlighting his enduring legacy as a champion of the oppressed and marginalized.

Dr. Ambedkar's influence extends beyond academic circles to the realm of activism and advocacy, where his ideas have inspired movements for social justice and equality in various parts of the world. From the civil rights movement in the United States to the anti-caste struggles in South Africa and beyond, Babasaheb's teachings have provided a framework for understanding and challenging systems of oppression and discrimination.

His emphasis on self-respect, dignity, and empowerment continues to resonate with marginalized communities around the world, inspiring them to assert their rights and demand justice.

As we explore the global reverberations of Dr. Ambedkar's ideas and legacy, we are reminded of the universality of his message and the enduring relevance of his teachings in the fight against injustice and inequality. Babasaheb's vision of a world free from caste-based discrimination and social hierarchy continues to inspire millions of people across borders and cultures, uniting them in the shared struggle for dignity, equality, and human rights.

Chapter 15
Continuing the Legacy

As we step into the 21st century, the vision and legacy of Dr. B.R. Ambedkar resonate more strongly than ever, serving as a guiding light for humanity in the pursuit of social justice, equality, and dignity for all. In a world grappling with persistent inequalities, deep-rooted prejudices, and systemic injustices, Babasaheb's teachings offer invaluable insights and inspiration for addressing the pressing challenges of our time.

At the core of Dr. Ambedkar's vision is the belief in the inherent worth and dignity of every human being, regardless of caste, creed, or background. In a world torn apart by divisions and disparities, Babasaheb's message of unity, solidarity, and respect for diversity serves as a powerful antidote to hatred and discrimination. His emphasis on social justice and equality reminds us of the imperative of building a more inclusive and equitable society, where every individual has the opportunity to fulfill their potential and lead a life of dignity and fulfillment.

In the 21st century, Dr. Ambedkar's legacy is more relevant than ever as we confront the complex challenges of globalization, technological advancement, and environmental degradation. His teachings on democracy, human rights, and social reform provide a roadmap for navigating these turbulent times, guiding us towards a future characterized by justice, compassion, and sustainability.

One of the key imperatives of continuing Dr. Ambedkar's legacy is the need to confront and dismantle systems of oppression and discrimination that continue to marginalize and exclude millions of people around the world. Whether it is caste-based discrimination in India, racial injustice in the United States, or systemic inequalities in access to education, healthcare, and economic opportunities globally, Babasaheb's teachings remind us of the moral imperative of standing up for the rights and dignity of the marginalized and oppressed.

Another crucial aspect of continuing Dr. Ambedkar's legacy is the promotion of education as a tool for empowerment and social transformation. Babasaheb recognized the transformative power of knowledge in challenging oppressive structures and empowering individuals to assert their rights and dignity. In the 21st century, we must work towards ensuring access to quality education for all, particularly for those from marginalized and disadvantaged backgrounds, so that they may realize their full potential and contribute meaningfully to society.

As we reflect on the enduring relevance of Dr. Ambedkar's vision and legacy in the 21st century, we are reminded of our collective responsibility to carry forward his unfinished agenda of social justice, equality, and dignity for all. Babasaheb's life and teachings continue to inspire generations of activists, scholars, and policymakers to strive for a world where every individual is treated with respect, dignity, and compassion—a world that reflects the true spirit of Babasaheb's vision of social justice and equality.

Chapter 16
Tribute to Babasaheb

Dr. B.R. Ambedkar's death marked the end of an era and the beginning of a new chapter in India's history. His passing on December 6, 1956, sent shockwaves across the nation and left a profound void in the hearts of millions who revered him as a beacon of hope and a champion of social justice.

Ambedkar's death came at a time when he was deeply engaged in the struggle for the rights and dignity of the marginalized communities he dedicated his life to serving. As the architect of India's Constitution and a tireless advocate for Dalit rights, his demise left a gaping hole in the fabric of Indian society, prompting an outpouring of grief and mourning from people of all walks of life.

The news of Ambedkar's passing spread rapidly, eliciting expressions of sorrow and tribute from far and wide. Across the length and breadth of India, millions mourned the loss of a leader whose legacy would endure for generations to come. From the bustling streets of Mumbai to the remote villages of rural India, people gathered to pay their respects to the departed soul, reflecting on his life's work and the indelible mark he left on the nation's conscience.

In the aftermath of his death, India witnessed an unprecedented outpouring of grief and solidarity. Dalits, who had found in Ambedkar a voice for their aspirations and a champion for their rights, mourned the loss of their beloved leader with deep sorrow and reverence. But beyond the Dalit community, people from all walks of life, irrespective of caste, creed, or background, came together to honor the memory of a man whose legacy transcended the boundaries of identity and ideology.

Ambedkar's funeral procession was a solemn and somber affair, as millions gathered to bid farewell to a leader who had dedicated his life to the cause of social justice and equality. His mortal remains were laid to rest at Chaitya Bhoomi, a memorial in Mumbai that would become a sacred pilgrimage site for millions of his followers in the years to come.

In the aftermath of his death, Ambedkar's legacy continued to reverberate throughout Indian society. His teachings and ideals inspired countless individuals and movements dedicated to carrying forward the struggle for social justice, equality, and human dignity. From grassroots activists to political leaders, from scholars to students, people across India and beyond took up the mantle of Ambedkar's unfinished agenda, pledging to work tirelessly towards building a more just, equitable, and inclusive society.

Today, more than six decades after his passing, Dr. B.R. Ambedkar remains an enduring symbol of hope and inspiration for millions of people around the world. His legacy lives on in the hearts and minds of all those who continue to strive for a world where every individual is treated with dignity, respect, and equality—a world that reflects the true spirit of Babasaheb's vision and ideals.

In the annals of history, there are few figures whose indomitable spirit and unwavering commitment to justice leave an enduring impact on humanity. Dr. B.R. Ambedkar, affectionately known as Babasaheb, stands tall among them, his life and teachings serving as a beacon of hope and inspiration for millions around the world.

Babasaheb's journey from the depths of social oppression to the corridors of power is a testament to the resilience of the human spirit and the power of determination in the face of adversity. Born into a society rife with discrimination and prejudice, Dr. Ambedkar defied the odds to become a towering figure in the fight for social justice and equality.

Throughout his life, Babasaheb confronted the forces of injustice and inequality with unwavering courage and conviction. From his relentless crusade against caste-based discrimination to his pivotal role in drafting the Indian Constitution, Dr. Ambedkar's contributions to the cause of human rights and dignity are immeasurable.

But Babasaheb's legacy extends far beyond his accomplishments as a scholar, statesman, and social reformer. It lies in the timeless principles of equality, justice, and human dignity that he espoused, principles that continue to resonate with people of all backgrounds and beliefs.

In the 21st century, Dr. Ambedkar's teachings remain as relevant as ever, offering invaluable insights into the challenges of our time and guiding us towards a more just, equitable, and inclusive society. His emphasis on education, empowerment, and social reform serves as a roadmap for confronting the systemic injustices that continue to plague our world.

As we pay homage to Babasaheb, we are reminded of the immense debt of gratitude we owe to him for his tireless efforts to uplift the oppressed and marginalized. His legacy is not merely a chapter in history but a living testament to the enduring power of hope, courage, and perseverance in the face of adversity.

In honoring Dr. Ambedkar, we reaffirm our commitment to carrying forward his unfinished agenda of social justice, equality, and human dignity. We strive to build a world where every individual is treated with respect and compassion, where opportunity knows no bounds, and where the promise of Babasaheb's vision of a casteless society is finally realized.

May we draw strength from Babasaheb's indomitable spirit and unwavering resolve as we continue on the journey towards a brighter, more just, and inclusive future for all.

Chapter 17
The Eternal Flame

In the tapestry of human history, there are rare souls whose brilliance illuminates the darkest corners of injustice and inequality, casting a radiant glow of hope and inspiration for generations to come. Dr. B.R. Ambedkar, affectionately known as Babasaheb, stands as one such luminary—a beacon of light whose immortal legacy continues to ignite the flames of social justice and equality in the hearts of all who champion the cause of human dignity.

Babasaheb's legacy is not bound by the confines of time or geography; it transcends borders and generations, leaving an indelible mark on modern India and the world. His teachings on democracy, human rights, and social reform continue to shape the discourse of justice and equality, resonating with millions who seek to build a more just, equitable, and inclusive society.

In modern India, Dr. Ambedkar's impact is palpable in every sphere of life, from politics and governance to education and social activism. His pivotal role in drafting the Indian Constitution laid the foundation for a democratic and pluralistic society, enshrining the principles of equality, liberty, and fraternity as the cornerstones of the nation's identity. Babasaheb's advocacy for affirmative action and social welfare programs has empowered millions of marginalized individuals to access opportunities for education, employment, and social mobility, thereby transforming lives and communities across the country.

But Dr. Ambedkar's influence extends far beyond the borders of India, resonating with people of all backgrounds and beliefs who share his vision of a world free from discrimination and oppression. From the civil rights movement in the United States to the anti-caste struggles in South Asia and beyond, Babasaheb's teachings serve as a guiding light for activists and advocates fighting for justice and equality in every corner of the globe.

What makes Dr. Ambedkar's legacy truly immortal is not just his remarkable achievements or his towering intellect, but the eternal flame of hope and inspiration that he ignites in the hearts of all who dare to dream of a better world. His unwavering commitment to the cause of social justice, his boundless compassion for the oppressed and marginalized, and his unyielding faith in the power of education and empowerment continue to inspire us to strive for a more just, equitable, and compassionate society.

As we conclude our journey through the life and legacy of Dr. B.R. Ambedkar, let us carry forward the torch of hope and inspiration that he has passed down to us. Let us draw strength from his indomitable spirit and unwavering resolve as we continue the noble pursuit of justice, equality, and human dignity—for in the eternal flame of Babasaheb's legacy, we find the guiding light that will lead us towards a brighter, more compassionate, and inclusive future for all.

Conclusion

As we come to the end of this journey through the life and legacy of Dr. B.R. Ambedkar, let us pause to reflect on the profound impact of his teachings and the enduring relevance of his vision in our world today.

Dr. Ambedkar's life was a testament to the power of courage, determination, and resilience in the face of adversity. Born into a society plagued by caste-based discrimination and social injustice, Babasaheb defied the odds to become a towering figure in the fight for equality, justice, and human dignity.

Throughout his life, Dr. Ambedkar championed the cause of the oppressed and marginalized, tirelessly advocating for their rights and empowerment. His seminal contributions to the drafting of the Indian Constitution laid the foundation for a democratic and inclusive society, while his unwavering commitment to social reform inspired generations to strive for a world free from discrimination and oppression.

But Babasaheb's legacy is not merely a chapter in history; it is a living testament to the enduring power of hope, compassion, and solidarity. His teachings continue to inspire millions around the world to stand up against injustice, to speak out for the voiceless, and to work towards a more just, equitable, and inclusive society.

In closing, let us reaffirm our commitment to the ideals espoused by Dr. B.R. Ambedkar and rededicate ourselves to the pursuit of a society where every individual is treated with dignity, respect, and equality. Let us draw inspiration from Babasaheb's indomitable spirit and unwavering resolve as we continue the noble journey towards a brighter, more compassionate, and inclusive future for all.

This book is a tribute to the life, legacy, and enduring spirit of Dr. Babasaheb Ambedkar—a beacon of hope, a harbinger of change, and an eternal inspiration to all. May his teachings guide us, his legacy inspire us, and his spirit uplift us as we strive to build a world that reflects the true spirit of justice, equality, and human dignity.

Special Summary: Dr. B.R. Ambedkar

Dr. Bhimrao Ramji Ambedkar, popularly known as Babasaheb, was a visionary leader, social reformer, and architect of modern India's democratic framework. His life and work continue to inspire generations around the world. Here's a special summary highlighting some of his most significant works, key dates, and enduring contributions:

Key Dates

- April 14, 1891: Birth of Bhimrao Ramji Ambedkar in Mhow, Madhya Pradesh.
- 1927: Mahad Satyagraha - A pivotal movement led by Dr. Ambedkar to assert Dalit rights to access public water sources.
- 1932: Signing of the Poona Pact - Negotiated by Dr. Ambedkar, securing reserved electoral seats for Dalits in British India.
- 1947: Appointment as Independent India's first Law Minister and Chairman of the Constitution Drafting Committee.
- January 26, 1950: Adoption of the Indian Constitution - A monumental achievement, reflecting Dr. Ambedkar's vision of a just and inclusive society.
- December 6, 1956: Conversion to Buddhism - Dr. Ambedkar embraced Buddhism, advocating it as a path to liberation from caste oppression.
- December 6, 1956: Establishment of the Buddha Dhamma Deeksha Bhoomi in Nagpur - A significant event symbolizing Dr. Ambedkar's commitment to Buddhism and social justice.

Important Works and Contributions

1. Annihilation of Caste: Dr. Ambedkar's seminal work challenges the caste system's deeply entrenched social hierarchies, advocating for its eradication to achieve true equality.

2. The Constitution of India: As Chairman of the Constitution Drafting Committee, Dr. Ambedkar played a pivotal role in shaping India's democratic principles, enshrining fundamental rights and social justice provisions.

3. Buddhist Conversion: Dr. Ambedkar's conversion to Buddhism signaled a powerful rejection of caste-based discrimination, offering millions of Dalits a path to spiritual emancipation and social equality.

4. Social and Educational Reforms: Babasaheb tirelessly campaigned for Dalit rights, advocating for affirmative action policies, access to education, and social welfare programs to uplift marginalized communities.

5. International Advocacy: Dr. Ambedkar represented India at international forums, advocating for minority rights and social justice on the global stage, leaving a lasting impact on the discourse of human rights worldwide.

Enduring Legacy

Dr. B.R. Ambedkar's legacy extends far beyond his lifetime, inspiring movements for social justice, equality, and human rights around the world. His teachings continue to guide millions in their quest for dignity, empowerment, and liberation from oppression. Babasaheb's vision of a just and inclusive society remains as relevant today as it was during his lifetime, urging us to strive towards a world where every individual is treated with respect, dignity, and equality.

Dr. B.R. Ambedkar's role in the Constitution of India was pivotal and multifaceted, shaping the foundational document of independent India in profound ways. Here's a detailed overview of his contributions:

1. Chairmanship of the Drafting Committee: Dr. Ambedkar was appointed as the Chairman of the Constitution Drafting Committee on August 29, 1947. As the head of this committee, he played a central role in drafting and finalizing the Constitution of India.
2. Architect of Fundamental Rights: One of Dr. Ambedkar's key contributions was his advocacy for fundamental rights. He championed the inclusion of fundamental rights in the Constitution to safeguard individual liberties and protect citizens from state tyranny.
3. Champion of Social Justice: Dr. Ambedkar's lifelong commitment to social justice found expression in the Constitution through provisions aimed at uplifting marginalized and oppressed communities. He advocated for affirmative action measures such as reservations in education, employment, and political representation to address historical injustices and ensure the equitable participation of all sections of society.
4. Advocate for Dalit Rights: As a Dalit leader, Dr. Ambedkar fought tirelessly for the rights of Dalits (formerly known as Untouchables).

He ensured that the Constitution included provisions to eradicate untouchability, promote social equality, and empower Dalits through affirmative action.

5. Defender of Minority Rights: Dr. Ambedkar emphasized the importance of protecting the rights of religious and cultural minorities in a diverse and pluralistic society. He advocated for provisions in the Constitution to safeguard minority interests and ensure their full participation in the democratic process.
6. Steward of Parliamentary Democracy: Dr. Ambedkar played a crucial role in shaping the structure and functioning of India's parliamentary democracy. He crafted provisions related to the composition and powers of the executive, legislature, and judiciary, laying the groundwork for India's democratic governance system.
7. Visionary Leadership: Beyond his specific contributions to the text of the Constitution, Dr. Ambedkar provided visionary leadership during the drafting process. He navigated complex political and social dynamics, bridged differences among various stakeholders, and steered the committee towards consensus, ensuring the adoption of a Constitution that reflected the aspirations of the people of India.

Dr. B.R. Ambedkar's role in the Constitution of India was not merely that of a legal draftsman but that of a visionary statesman and social reformer. His enduring legacy as the principal architect of India's Constitution continues to inspire generations, underscoring the transformative power of law in advancing the cause of justice, equality, and democracy.

Here are some lesser-known facts about Dr. B.R. Ambedkar

1. Polyglot Scholar: Dr. Ambedkar was proficient in several languages, including Marathi, Hindi, English, Sanskrit, Pali, and Persian. His linguistic skills enabled him to engage with a wide range of texts and cultures, shaping his intellectual breadth and depth.
2. First Dalit to Obtain a Doctorate: Dr. Ambedkar earned his Ph.D. in Economics from Columbia University in 1927, becoming the first Dalit to achieve this academic milestone. His doctoral thesis, titled "The Evolution of Provincial Finance in British India," showcased his scholarly acumen and analytical prowess.
3. Published Author: Beyond his academic achievements, Dr. Ambedkar was a prolific writer and published author. He wrote extensively on a wide range of subjects, including economics, sociology, history, and politics, contributing significantly to Indian intellectual discourse.

4. Legal Luminary: Dr. Ambedkar was one of India's foremost legal minds, earning recognition for his expertise in law and jurisprudence. He practiced law in both India and the United Kingdom, specializing in labor and constitutional law.
5. Iconic Public Speaker: Dr. Ambedkar was renowned for his eloquence and oratorical skills. He delivered powerful speeches that galvanized audiences and inspired millions to join the struggle for social justice and equality.
6. Pioneer of Women's Rights: Dr. Ambedkar was a staunch advocate for gender equality and women's rights. He championed reforms to eradicate practices such as child marriage and advocated for women's education and empowerment.
7. Emancipation through Education: Dr. Ambedkar believed in the transformative power of education as a means of social emancipation. He established educational institutions such as the People's Education Society to provide access to quality education for marginalized communities.
8. Symbol of Dalit Assertion: Dr. Ambedkar's conversion to Buddhism in 1956 marked a significant moment in Dalit history. It symbolized a rejection of caste-based discrimination and a reaffirmation of Dalit identity and dignity.
9. Architect of Labour Reforms: Dr. Ambedkar played a key role in shaping labor laws in India. As the first Labor Minister of independent India, he introduced significant reforms to protect the rights and welfare of workers, including minimum wages, social security, and labor rights legislation.
10. Legacy of Statues: Dr. Ambedkar's legacy is commemorated through numerous statues and memorials erected across India and around the world. These monuments serve as symbols of his enduring influence and inspire future generations to carry forward his mission of social justice and equality.

These lesser-known facts offer glimpses into the multifaceted persona and profound contributions of Dr. B.R. Ambedkar, illuminating the breadth and depth of his impact on Indian society and beyond.

While Dr. B.R. Ambedkar's life and contributions are extensively documented, there are a few aspects that remain shrouded in mystery or subject to speculation. Here are some intriguing mysteries surrounding him:

1. Early Childhood and Family Origins: Despite being a pivotal figure in Indian history, there are limited details available about Dr. Ambedkar's early childhood and family origins. The specifics

of his ancestry and the circumstances of his upbringing before his formal education are relatively unknown.

2. Personal Life and Relationships: Dr. Ambedkar's personal life and relationships are relatively mysterious, with few records shedding light on his private affairs. Little is known about his romantic interests, if any, or his experiences with familial relationships beyond his immediate family.
3. Unpublished Works and Manuscripts: While Dr. Ambedkar was a prolific writer and published author, there may be unpublished works or manuscripts that have yet to be discovered or made public. These potential writings could offer valuable insights into his thoughts, perspectives, and unpublished research.
4. Spiritual and Philosophical Evolution: Dr. Ambedkar's conversion to Buddhism in 1956 marked a significant turning point in his life, but the intricacies of his spiritual and philosophical evolution remain somewhat enigmatic. The precise reasons behind his embrace of Buddhism and the depth of his spiritual beliefs warrant further exploration.
5. International Connections and Influence: Dr. Ambedkar's international connections and influence are intriguing but relatively understudied. While he engaged with international forums and advocated for minority rights on the global stage, the extent of his interactions with international leaders and the impact of his ideas beyond India's borders merit further investigation.
6. Economic and Policy Perspectives: Despite his significant contributions to economics and policy formulation in India, there may be aspects of Dr. Ambedkar's economic and policy perspectives that are not fully understood or appreciated. Delving deeper into his economic theories and policy recommendations could reveal additional layers of insight.
7. Contemporary Relevance and Interpretations: The enduring relevance of Dr. Ambedkar's ideas and legacy in contemporary contexts remains a subject of debate and interpretation. Unraveling the mysteries surrounding how his teachings are interpreted, applied, and adapted by different individuals and communities today could provide valuable insights into his ongoing impact.

While these mysteries add layers of intrigue to Dr. Ambedkar's life and legacy they also underscore the importance of continued research, scholarship, and exploration to unravel the complexities of his remarkable journey and enduring influence.

From The Author

"As I bid farewell to the pages of this book, I am reminded of the timeless words of Dr. B.R. Ambedkar: 'Life should be great rather than long.' In chronicling the life and legacy of this extraordinary visionary, may we be inspired to embrace greatness in our own lives, to stand up for justice, to champion equality, and to strive relentlessly for a world where every individual is treated with dignity and respect. As the author of this book, I am humbled to have had the opportunity to share the remarkable story of Dr. Ambedkar, and I hope that his journey will continue to illuminate our path towards a brighter, more inclusive future for all. Thank you for joining me on this transformative journey."

- ASHOK M